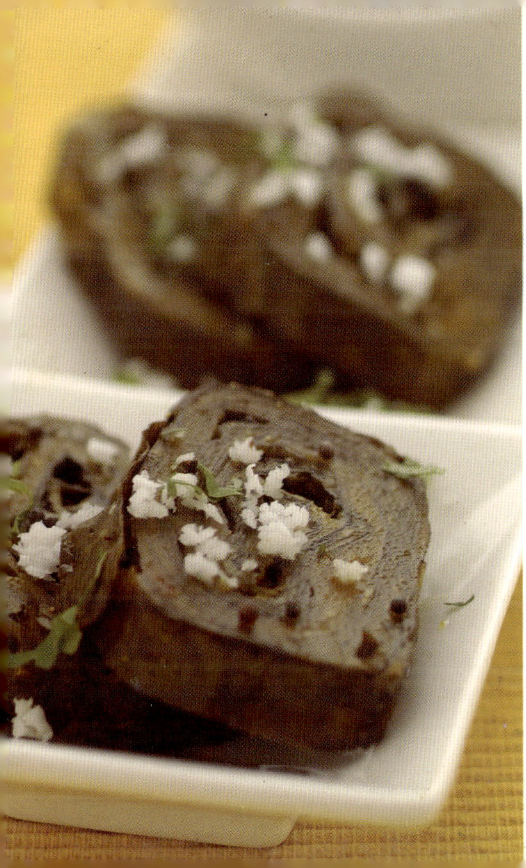

GREEN

In association with Alyona Kapoor

www.popularprakashan.com

Published by
POPULAR PRAKASHAN PVT. LTD.
301, Mahalaxmi Chambers
22, Bhulabhai Desai Road
Mumbai - 400 026
for Khana Khazana Publications Pvt. Ltd.

© 2010 Sanjeev Kapoor
First Published July 2010
Second Reprint September 2011

WORLD RIGHTS RESERVED. The contents – all recipes, photographs and drawings are original and copyrighted. No portion of this book shall be reproduced, stored in a retrieval system or transmitted by any means, electronic, mechanical, photocopying, recording or otherwise, without the written permission of the author and the publisher.

(4361)
ISBN: 978-81-7991-613-1

Design: Anjali Sawant
Photography: Bharat Bhirangi

PRINTED IN INDIA
by Rave India
A-27, Naraina Industrial Area, Phase II
New Delhi 110028

AUTHOR'S NOTE

Green is in! Be it our lifestyle and environmental choices, and now our food choices too!

Green leafy vegetables are powerhouses of nutrition as they are rich in vitamins and minerals like iron and calcium. While we have always known they are good for health, the trick is to make them taste lip-smacking and delicious.

And you will find out how to do just that in this collection of traditional, Indian-style main dishes and breads, as well as light and healthy international salads and bakes. The recipes feature spinach, fenugreek, lettuce, radish, and mustard leaves, among others.

Enjoy the hearty Sarson da Saag, and the tempting Methi Tomato Paneer. Indulge in the rustic Mooli ki Sabzi and go light with a refreshing Pineapple and Lettuce Salad, or the comforting warmth of the Spinach and Potato Soup.

'Eat your greens!' is what our mothers have always been telling us! It's time we listened.

Happy cooking!

CONTENTS

SOUPS AND SALADS

Spinach and Rice Soup	6
Lettuce and Cottage Cheese Broth	8
Toasted Almond and Spinach Soup	9
Fattoush	10
Kimchi	12
California Salad	13
Classic Greek Salad	14
Christmas Coleslaw	15
Pineapple and Lettuce Salad	16
Coleslaw with Cottage Cheese	18
Green Jewels in a Bowl	19
Leafy Greens with Vinaigrette	20

SNACKS

Spinach and Cheese Idli	22
Besan Cheela with Stuffed Methi	23
Methi Khakra	26
Spinach and Mushroom Pancakes	27
Cheeley Poode	29
Patra	30
Palak Puri with Tamatar Aloo	32
Patrado	34
Palak Pakore ki Chaat	36
Crackling Spinach	38
Spinach-stuffed Chillies	40

MAIN COURSE

Maatachi Bhaji	41
Palak-Baby Corn Sabzi	42
Aluchi Patal Bhaji	43

Spinach Gnocchi	46
Mooli ki Sabzi	49
Paneer Kofte in Spinach Curry	50
Methi Aloo	52
Chinese Greens with Soy Sauce	54
Mooli Saag	56
Spinach and Potato Bhaji	58
Methi Tamatar Paneer	59
Soppina Palya	60
Moolyachi Bhaji	61
Chakvatachi Bhaji	62
Sarson da Saag	63
Cabbage with Chana Dal	65
Sai Bhaji	66
Steamed Lauki and Palak Kofte	68
Methiwali Arhar Dal	70
Palak ki Kadhi	72
Keerai Milakootal	74
Palakwali Dal	76

RICE AND BREAD

Methi Chaman Biryani	78
Methi Makai Biryani	82
Spinach and Mushroom Risotto	84
Tiranga Kofta Pulao	86
Palak aur Paneer Parantha	89
Methi Makai Parantha	91

Annexure 94
Glossary 96

SPINACH AND RICE SOUP

400 grams spinach, blanched and puréed

¼ cup arborio rice, soaked

2 tablespoons olive oil

1 small onion, chopped

2 garlic cloves, chopped

1 small fresh red chilli, seeded and chopped

6 cups Vegetable Stock (page 95)

Salt to taste

10-12 black peppercorns, freshly ground

4 tablespoons grated Parmesan cheese

- Heat the olive oil in a large non-stick pan; add the onion, garlic and red chilli, and sauté for about five minutes or until softened.
- Drain the rice and add to the pan. Stir well, add the vegetable stock and bring to a boil.
- Lower the heat and simmer for another ten minutes.
- Add the spinach purée, salt and the freshly ground peppercorns, and cook for five minutes or till the rice is tender.
- Serve hot, garnished with the grated Parmesan cheese.

LETTUCE AND COTTAGE CHEESE BROTH

20 romaine lettuce leaves, roughly torn

150 grams cottage cheese, cut into ½-inch cubes

1 medium carrot, peeled and thinly sliced

2 spring onions with greens

1 inch ginger, finely chopped

1½ teaspoons refined oil

4 cups Vegetable Stock (page 95)

1 tablespoon soy sauce

2 tablespoons dry sherry

1 teaspoon sugar

Salt to taste

Black pepper powder to taste

1 teaspoon red chilli flakes

1 teaspoon vinegar

- Wash and cut the spring onion bulbs into slices. Chop the spring onion greens. Heat a non-stick pan and sauté the cottage cheese in a little oil on high heat until golden brown. Remove from the pan and place on absorbent paper.
- Heat the remaining oil in the same pan and sauté the sliced spring onion bulbs, carrot and ginger for half a minute. Add the vegetable stock and bring to a boil. Stir in the soy sauce and dry sherry, and season with the sugar, salt and thr pepper powder.
- Add the cottage cheese and the lettuce and stir gently to mix. Stir in the red chilli flakes and vinegar. Serve piping hot, garnished with the spring onion greens.

TOASTED ALMOND AND SPINACH SOUP

¼ cup almonds, toasted and slivered

400 grams spinach, shredded

1 tablespoon oil

1 bay leaf

1 medium onion, chopped

5 garlic cloves, chopped

6-8 black peppercorns

Salt to taste

1 cup milk

- Heat the oil in a non-stick pan; add the bay leaf, onion, garlic and peppercorns, and sauté for a few seconds. Reserve some shredded spinach for garnishing, and add the rest to the pan. Sauté for four to five minutes.
- Add three cups of water and salt. Bring the mixture to a boil and cook for a minute longer. Take the pan off the heat and strain the mixture. Reserve the cooking liquid. When slightly cooled, purée the spinach in a blender.
- Transfer the purée to a non-stick pan, add the reserved cooking liquid and mix. Add the milk, adjust the seasoning and bring the mixture to a boil.
- Place the shredded spinach in four individual soup bowls and pour the hot soup over. Garnish with the almond slivers and serve immediately.

FATTOUSH

- 1 medium green capsicum, cut into 1-inch cubes
- 1 medium tomato, cut into 1-inch pieces
- 1 medium cucumber, cut into 1-inch pieces
- 1 medium onion, cut into 1-inch pieces
- 2 tablespoons olive oil
- 2-3 bread slices, cut into 1-inch cubes
- 1 small head of iceberg lettuce, roughly torn
- 5-6 black olives, stoned
- 5-6 green olives, stoned
- 1-2 sprigs fresh parsley

Dressing
- 3 tablespoons olive oil
- 1 tablespoon vinegar
- 1 tablespoon lemon juice
- Salt to taste
- ½ teaspoon black peppercorns, crushed
- 1 tablespoon fresh parsley, roughly torn
- 1 teaspoon dried mint

- Heat the olive oil in a non-stick pan; add the bread cubes and sauté over medium heat to make golden croutons.
- To make the dressing, pour the olive oil into a bowl; add the vinegar, lemon juice, salt, crushed peppercorns, parsley and dried mint, and whisk well.

- In a large bowl, mix together the lettuce, all the vegetables, and the olives. Add the parsley and toss well to mix.
- Just before serving, pour the dressing over the salad, add the croutons and toss again. Serve immediately.

KIMCHI

1 small cabbage, cut into 1-inch pieces

2 tablespoons sesame oil

4 teaspoons brown sugar

1 teaspoon soy sauce

2 tablespoons vinegar

3 teaspoons crushed red chillies

Salt to taste

½ teaspoon roasted sesame seeds

- Heat the sesame oil in a non-stick pan. Add the brown sugar, soy sauce, vinegar, crushed red chillies and salt. Add the cabbage and turn off the heat.
- Toss well to mix. Sprinkle the sesame seeds and serve.

CALIFORNIA SALAD

1 large head of lettuce, roughly torn and soaked in chilled water

4 medium carrots, coarsely grated

18-20 cherry tomatoes, halved

4 celery stalks, thinly sliced

1 cup seedless raisins

1 cup almonds, blanched and halved

4 tablespoons *chironji*

2 tablespoons roasted sesame seeds

Salt to taste

15-20 black peppercorns, freshly ground

Dressing

3 tablespoons extra virgin olive oil

2 tablespoons cider vinegar

2 teaspoons honey

4 tablespoons orange juice

- Place all the vegetables, raisins, almonds, *chironji* and sesame seeds in a large bowl. Place all the dressing ingredients in a small glass jar, close tightly and shake well to mix.
- Pour the dressing over the salad and toss well to mix. Serve chilled, sprinkled with the salt and the freshly ground peppercorns.

CLASSIC GREEK SALAD

1 head of iceberg lettuce, roughly torn

1 medium cucumber, halved lengthways and sliced

4 medium tomatoes, cut into wedges

8 spring onions, sliced

10 black olives, stoned

100 grams feta cheese, diced

Dressing

3 tablespoons white vinegar

2 tablespoons extra virgin olive oil

Salt to taste

10-12 black peppercorns, freshly ground

- Place the lettuce, cucumber, tomatoes, spring onions, olives and cheese in a large bowl.
- For the dressing, whisk together the vinegar and olive oil in a small bowl. Add the salt and ground peppercorns.
- Pour the dressing over the salad and toss well to mix.
- Serve immediately with crusty bread.

CHRISTMAS COLESLAW

1 small green cabbage, shredded
1 small purple cabbage, shredded
3 tablespoons crushed walnut kernels
½ cup Mayonnaise (page 95)
1 tablespoon French Dressing (page 94)

Salt to taste
$1/8$ teaspoon white pepper powder
2-inch celery stalk, chopped
½ medium apple, cut into thin strips

- Place the shredded cabbages and two tablespoons of the crushed walnuts in a large bowl.
- In a separate bowl, mix together the mayonnaise with the French dressing, salt, white pepper powder and celery.
- Pour the dressing over the cabbage mixture. Add the apple and toss gently to mix.
- Serve, sprinkled with the remaining crushed walnuts.

PINEAPPLE AND LETTUCE SALAD

6 pineapple slices, cut into ¾–inch pieces

16-20 iceberg lettuce leaves, torn into bite-sized pieces

2 medium cucumbers, peeled, halved lengthways and seeded

2 tablespoons lemon juice

3 tablespoons pineapple juice

1 tablespoon honey

Salt to taste

¼ teaspoon dried mixed herbs

1 teaspoon crushed peppercorns

¼ teaspoon white pepper powder

- Wash and soak the iceberg lettuce in ice cold water for about fifteen minutes.
- Cut the cucumbers into three-fourth inch pieces.
- Mix together the lemon juice, pineapple juice, honey, salt, mixed herbs, crushed peppercorns and white pepper powder. Set aside for at least fifteen minutes.
- Combine the lettuce, pineapple and cucumbers in a bowl.
- Pour the dressing over the salad and toss lightly. Serve immediately.

COLESLAW WITH COTTAGE CHEESE

1 small cabbage, shredded
2 medium carrots, grated
100 grams cottage cheese, crumbled
½ cup drained (hung) yogurt
Salt to taste
¼ teaspoon mustard powder

½ teaspoon white pepper powder
½ teaspoon sugar
¼ teaspoon caraway seeds
½ cup milk
1 tablespoon lemon juice
1 medium onion, grated

- Place the cottage cheese, drained yogurt, salt, mustard powder, white pepper powder, sugar and caraway seeds in a blender and process till smooth. Add the milk and process again.
- Place the cabbage in a bowl. Add the salt, lemon juice and carrots, and mix well.
- Squeeze out the water from the grated onion and add to the cabbage.
- Add the cottage cheese dressing and toss to mix.
- Serve immediately.

GREEN JEWELS IN A BOWL

¼ medium broccoli, separated into florets

1 medium green capsicum, cut into strips

1 large cucumber, halved and sliced diagonally

8-10 French beans, sliced diagonally, and blanched

¾ cup bean sprouts

6 lettuce leaves, roughly torn and chilled

1 stalk spring onion greens, sliced

1 tablespoon roasted sesame seeds

Dressing

1 tablespoon lemon juice

1 tablespoon olive oil

1 tablespoon soy sauce

3 teaspoons powdered sugar

7-8 black peppercorns, crushed

Salt to taste

- Blanch the broccoli florets in boiling water. Refresh in cold water. Mix together the ingredients for the dressing and set aside.
- Place the broccoli, capsicum, cucumber, French beans, bean sprouts and lettuce in a large bowl. Pour the dressing over the salad and toss well to mix.
- Serve, sprinkled with the spring onion greens and roasted sesame seeds.

LEAFY GREENS WITH VINAIGRETTE

¼ small cabbage, cut into 1-inch pieces

1 medium head of iceberg lettuce

1 head of romaine lettuce

16-20 tender spinach leaves

8-10 tender radish leaves

½ cup dill leaves

Dressing

½ cup (120 ml) apple juice

1 teaspoon caraway seeds, roasted and crushed

1 tablespoon olive oil

4 tablespoons red wine vinegar

¼ teaspoon paprika or red chilli powder

1 teaspoon honey

½ teaspoon crushed black pepper

Salt to taste

- Place all the ingredients for the dressing in a bottle, close tightly and shake well to mix. Refrigerate till required.
- Trim and wash the lettuce, spinach, radish and dill leaves in plenty of water. Refresh in chilled water.
- Tear the leaves into bite-size pieces, mix well and refrigerate to keep them crisp.
- Just before serving, pour the prepared dressing over the leaves and toss well.
- Serve chilled.

Chef's Tip

If red wine vinegar is not available, use malt vinegar instead.

SPINACH AND CHEESE IDLI

8-10 spinach leaves
¼ cup grated processed cheese
½ cup split black gram

1 cup *idli rawa*
Salt to taste
½ teaspoon crushed black peppercorns

- Soak the split black gram and *idli rawa* separately for three to four hours. Drain and grind the split black gram, sprinkling water as required, to make a smooth, spongy batter.
- Drain the *idli rawa* and add it with the salt to the split black gram batter and mix thoroughly with your hands, using a whipping motion so that the batter is mixed well. Place the batter in a large pan or bowl, cover tightly and place in a warm place for six hours, or at least overnight.
- Blanch the spinach leaves in boiling water for two to three minutes. Shred and reserve a few leaves and purée the rest. Add the spinach purée to the *idli* batter and mix well. Pour into lightly-oiled *idli* moulds, top with the shredded spinach leaves and grated cheese. Sprinkle crushed peppercorns and steam till the *idli* are done.
- Serve the *idli* with chilli sauce or chilli-garlic sauce.

BESAN CHEELA WITH STUFFED METHI

Cheela
2 cups gram flour

¼ teaspoon soda bicarbonate

Salt to taste

1 teaspoon red chilli powder

1 teaspoon carom seeds

A pinch of asafoetida

2 tablespoons chopped fresh coriander

Stuffing
1 cup fresh fenugreek leaves, chopped

2 medium onions, chopped

8-10 fresh button mushrooms, sliced

2½ cups grated cottage cheese

Salt to taste

¼ teaspoon black pepper powder

- For the stuffing, heat a non-stick *kadai* and roast the onions for two minutes. Add the fenugreek leaves and cook for another minute.
- Add the mushrooms, stir and cook till all the water dries up. Add the cottage cheese, salt and pepper powder; mix well and set aside to cool.

- In a bowl, mix together the gram flour, soda bicarbonate, salt, chilli powder, carom seeds, asafoetida, chopped coriander and sufficient water to make a batter of pouring consistency. Whisk well to ensure there are no lumps.
- Heat a non-stick *tawa*; pour a ladleful of batter and spread it evenly. Cook the *cheela* on both sides.
- Place a portion of the stuffing in the centre and fold the edges over it.
- Serve immediately.

METHI KHAKRA

1 teaspoon dried fenugreek leaves
2 cups wholewheat flour
Salt to taste
¼ teaspoon tumeric powder
1 teaspoon cumin powder
1 teaspoon ginger-green chilli paste

- Mix together the flour and the salt in a bowl. Add the tumeric powder, cumin powder, ginger-green chilli paste and dried fenugreek leaves, and mix well. Add enough water and knead into a medium soft dough.
- Divide the dough into twelve equal balls. Roll out each ball into very thin, round *chapati*. Heat a non-stick *tawa*, place a *chapati* on it and roast on low heat.
- Turn and press the *chapati* with a wooden press. Continue pressing and turning till the *khakra* is evenly cooked on both the sides.
- The *khakra* is done when it is light brown and crisp. Remove from heat, allow to cool and store in an airtight container, handling it carefully as it is crisp and may break.

SPINACH AND MUSHROOM PANCAKES

Pancakes

¾ cup wholewheat flour

1 cup + 2 tablespoons milk

Salt to taste

¼ teaspoon white pepper powder

¼ teaspoon carom seeds

½ teaspoon oil

1 cup grated processed cheese

2 medium tomatoes, sliced

Stuffing

20-25 large spinach leaves, roughly chopped

8-10 fresh button mushrooms, coarsely ground

1 teaspoon oil

1 medium onion, chopped

Salt to taste

¼ teaspoon white pepper powder

6-8 garlic cloves, chopped

- To make the stuffing, heat the oil and sauté the onion for thirty seconds. Add the mushrooms and continue to cook till almost dry. Add the spinach and cook till dry.
- Add the salt and white pepper powder to taste, stir in the garlic, remove from heat and keep warm.

- For the batter, place the wholewheat flour in a bowl. Add one cup of milk, the salt, white pepper powder and carom seeds. Whisk well to make a smooth batter.
- Heat a six-inch non-stick pan and grease lightly. Pour half a ladleful of the batter and spread into a three-inch round with the back of the ladle. Cook for half a minute over medium heat, turn over and cook for a few seconds.
- Spread a portion of the cooked spinach on three-fourth of each pancake.
- Spread some of the grated cheese and top with a few tomato slices. Roll up the pancake ensuring that the filling does not spill out. Use three-fourth cup of grated cheese for the filling.
- Preheat an oven to $220^0C/425^0F$/Gas Mark 7.
- Place the pancakes in a baking dish, sprinkle with the remaining grated cheese and two tablespoons of milk. Bake till the cheese melts. Serve immediately.

CHEELEY POODE

2 cups gram flour
½ cup fenugreek leaves
Salt to taste
¼ teaspoon turmeric powder
1 teaspoon red chilli powder
½ teaspoon *chaat masala*

1 tablespoon lemon juice
1 medium onion, chopped
Oil for shallow-frying
1 cup grated cottage cheese
½ cup grated cheese
1 teaspoon red chilli powder

- Combine the gram flour, fenugreek leaves, salt, turmeric powder, chilli powder, *chaat masala*, lemon juice and onion in a bowl. Stir in three-fourth cup of water to make a moderately thick batter.
- Heat a non-stick *tawa* and add a little oil. Pour a ladleful of batter and spread it evenly. Cook over low heat till the *cheeley* is cooked on one side. Drizzle some oil around the sides and over the top.
- Place some grated cottage cheese in the centre of the *cheeley*. Sprinkle with the grated cheese and chilli powder. Fold the two sides over the stuffing and serve hot.

PATRA

12 colocasia leaves
1½ cups gram flour
2 teaspoons coriander powder
1 teaspoon cumin powder
1 teaspoon red chilli powder
1 teaspoon turmeric powder
2 teaspoons sesame seeds
Salt to taste
1 teaspoon green chilli paste
1 teaspoon ginger paste
4 tablespoons oil
2 tablespoons tamarind pulp
3½ tablespoons grated jaggery
1 teaspoon mustard seeds

A pinch of asafoetida
¼ cup grated coconut
4 tablespoons chopped fresh coriander

- Remove the thick stems from the colocasia leaves. Wash the leaves, wipe them dry and set aside. Mix together the gram flour, coriander powder, cumin powder, chilli powder and turmeric powder in a bowl. Add the sesame seeds, salt, green chilli paste, ginger paste and two tablespoons of oil, and mix well. Mix together the tamarind pulp and jaggery, and add to the gram flour mixture.

- Place a leaf, shiny side down, on a work surface. Spread the paste evenly over the back of the leaf. Place another leaf over it, with its tapering end in the opposite direction of the first one. Spread some paste over it. Fold in the four edges and gently roll into a tight cylinder. Repeat the same with the rest of the leaves and paste. Place the rolls on a perforated plate or a sieve.

- Heat some water in a pressure cooker and place a metal ring or trivet in it. Place the sieve on the ring and seal the cooker with the lid. Steam without the weight for about twenty-five to thirty minutes, or till cooked. Insert a thin knife into the *patra* to check for doneness. If the knife comes out clean, the *patra* is cooked. Remove the *patra* and leave to cool. Cut into quarter-inch thick slices.

- Heat the remaining oil in a non-stick *kadai*; add the mustard seeds. When they begin to splutter, add the asafoetida and the slices of *patra*. Sauté till golden brown. Serve hot, garnished with coconut and chopped coriander.

PALAK PURI WITH TAMATAR ALOO

Palak Puri

15-20 large spinach leaves, blanched and puréed

1½ cups wholewheat flour

Salt to taste

1 tablespoon oil + for deep-frying

Tamatar Aloo

2 large tomatoes, chopped

4 medium unpeeled potatoes, diced

2 tablespoons oil

1 teaspoon cumin seeds

1 inch ginger, chopped

½ teaspoon turmeric powder

1 teaspoon coriander powder

½ teaspoon cumin powder

1 teaspoon red chilli powder

Salt to taste

- Mix the spinach purée with the wholewheat flour; add salt and one tablespoon of oil and knead into a moderately firm dough. Cover the dough with a damp cloth and leave to rest for about ten minutes. Divide into sixteen equal balls and roll into four-inch round *puri*.

- Heat sufficient oil in a *kadai* and deep-fry the *puri* over medium heat. Drain on absorbent paper and serve hot with *tamatar aloo*.
- To make the *tamatar aloo*, heat the oil in a non-stick pan; add the cumin seeds and tomatoes, and sauté for a few minutes. Add the ginger and continue to sauté for a while.
- Add the potatoes, turmeric powder, coriander powder, cumin powder, chilli powder and salt. Stir to mix and add two and a half cups of water.
- Cover and cook over low heat till the potatoes are tender.

PATRADO

12 medium colocasia leaves
1 cup split pigeon peas
½ cup rice
1 lemon-sized ball tamarind, soaked
10 Bedgi red chillies
A pinch of asafoetida

1 tablespoon grated jaggery
Salt to taste

Seasoning

2 tablespoons oil
½ teaspoon mustard seeds

- Soak the split pigeon peas and rice together for three to four hours. Drain.
- Grind together the pigeon peas, rice, tamarind, red chillies and asafoetida to a coarse paste using very little water.
- Add the grated jaggery and salt to taste and grind again to make a thick paste. Transfer to a bowl, cover and set aside for three to four hours.
- Remove the stalks of the colocasia leaves. Place a leaf on the worktop, shiny side facing downwards. Spread some *masala* evenly all over. Place another leaf over it

with its tapering end in the opposite direction of the first one. Spread some more *masala* over it. Similarly, place two more leaves, one over the other, spreading with the *masala* in between.

- Fold the sides of the leaves inwards and tightly roll up. Tie it up with a string. Similarly, make rolls with the remaining leaves and the *masala*.
- Heat the water in a steamer. Place the rolls in a shallow non-stick pan and place it in the steamer. Cover and steam for fifteen to twenty minutes or till the leaves turn a lighter shade.
- Allow the rolls to cool. Remove the strings. Cut into half-inch thick round slices.
- Heat the oil in a non-stick frying pan and add the mustard seeds. When the seeds start to splutter, place the slices in a single layer in the oil. Shallow-fry over medium heat till lightly browned on both the sides. Serve hot.

***Note:** Alternatively you can deep-fry the patrado slices till light brown. Drain and serve hot.*

PALAK PAKORE KI CHAAT

16-20 medium spinach leaves

1½ cups coarsely ground gram flour

Salt to taste

½ teaspoon red chilli powder

¼ teaspoon turmeric powder

½ teaspoon carom seeds

A pinch of asafoetida

Oil for deep-frying

1 cup yogurt

2 teaspoons roasted cumin seed powder

4 tablespoons Green Chutney (page 94)

4 tablespoons Date and Tamarind Chutney (page 94)

3 medium onions, chopped

½ cup *sev*

½ cup chopped fresh coriander

- Place the gram flour in a bowl with the salt, chilli powder, turmeric powder, carom seeds and asafoetida. Add enough water to make a thin batter.
- Heat sufficient oil in a *kadai*. Coat both the sides of each spinach leaf with the batter and deep-fry in hot oil till golden brown and crisp. Drain on absorbent paper.
- Whisk the yogurt with salt to taste.
- To serve, place two *palak pakore* on each serving plate. Cover with two to three tablespoons of whisked yogurt and sprinkle with roasted cumin powder. Top with dollops of green chutney and date and tamarind chutney.
- Sprinkle a little chopped onion and cover liberally with *sev*. Garnish with chopped coriander and serve immediately.

CRACKLING SPINACH

45 spinach leaves

Oil for deep-frying

1 tablespoon sesame oil

1 teaspoon red chilli flakes

Salt to taste

1 tablespoon sugar

1 tablespoon sesame seeds, toasted

- Trim, wash, drain and pat the spinach leaves dry. Cut into thin strips.
- Heat sufficient oil in a wok; add the spinach and deep-fry till crisp. Drain on absorbent paper.
- Heat the sesame oil in a non-stick wok; add the red chilli flakes and immediately add the fried spinach. Sprinkle salt to taste, sugar and toasted sesame seeds.
- Toss well to mix. Serve immediately.

Chef's Tip
As spinach has a high water content, first add a small quantity of spinach to stabilise the temperature of the oil before adding the rest.

SPINACH-STUFFED CHILLIES

12-16 large green chillies, slit and seeded

100 grams spinach, blanched and chopped

1 teaspoon oil

1 medium onion, finely chopped

½ cup fresh button mushrooms, chopped

½ teaspoon cumin powder

½ teaspoon red chilli powder

Salt to taste

¼ cup breadcrumbs

50 grams processed cheese, grated

Oil for greasing

- Heat the oil in a non-stick pan on medium heat; add the chopped onion and cook, stirring continuously, till the onion turns light golden brown. Add the chopped mushrooms and cook for another two to three minutes, stirring frequently.

- Add the spinach and cook for two minutes longer. Add the cumin powder, chilli powder and salt, and mix well. Remove from heat and cool.

- Add the breadcrumbs and grated cheese to the mixture. Stuff the green chillies with the spinach and mushroom mixture.

- Place the stuffed chillies in a baking dish and bake in a preheated oven at 200°C/400°F/Gas Mark 6 for about twenty minutes or until the chillies are soft. Serve hot.

MAATACHI BHAJI

1 bunch amaranth leaves, finely shredded
¼ cup peanuts
2 tablespoons oil
5-6 garlic cloves, finely chopped
1 medium onion, finely chopped
4-5 green chillies, finely chopped
¼ teaspoon turmeric powder
2 tablespoons gram flour
Salt to taste

- Roast the peanuts and crush them roughly.
- Heat the oil in a non-stick pan; add the garlic and sauté for a few seconds. Add the chopped onion and sauté till light brown.
- Add the green chillies, turmeric powder and shredded amaranth leaves; sprinkle a little water and cook for a few minutes.
- Mix together the gram flour and a little water and add to the pan. Add the peanuts and salt, and mix well. Cook for another five to six minutes, stirring frequently.
- Serve hot.

Note: *Maat is the Marathi word for amaranth leaves.*

PALAK-BABY CORN SABZI

450 grams spinach, chopped

10-12 pieces of baby corn, blanched and cut into ½-inch pieces

2 tablespoons oil

2 medium onions, cut into 1-inch cubes

5-6 garlic cloves, chopped

2-3 green chillies, slit

1 medium capsicum, cut into 1-inch cubes

2 tablespoons cornflour

¾ cup Vegetable Stock (page 95)

Salt to taste

¼ teaspoon MSG (optional)

¼ teaspoon black pepper powder

- Heat the oil in a non-stick pan. Add the onions and garlic, and cook for two minutes.
- Add the green chillies, capsicum and baby corn, and cook over a high heat for two to three minutes.
- Add the spinach and toss to mix. Add the cornflour, mixed with the vegetable stock and cook, stirring continuously, for two to three minutes.
- Stir in the salt, MSG and pepper powder. Serve hot.

ALUCHI PATAL BHAJI

8 colocasia leaves, shredded

¼ cup split Bengal gram, soaked

Salt to taste

3 tablespoons Tamarind Pulp (page 95)

3 tablespoons oil

½ teaspoon mustard seeds

5-6 curry leaves

A generous pinch of asafoetida

¼ teaspoon fenugreek seeds

4 garlic cloves, finely chopped

4-5 green chillies, finely chopped

¼ teaspoon turmeric powder

3 tablespoons gram flour

¼ cup raw peanuts, shelled

1 tablespoon grated jaggery

½ cup grated coconut

- Place the colocasia leaves in a non-stick pan, add four cups of water, salt, one and a half tablespoons of tamarind pulp and split Bengal gram, and boil till the *dal* is cooked.
- Heat the oil in another non-stick pan; add the mustard seeds, curry leaves, asafoetida, fenugreek seeds and garlic, and sauté for one minute.

- Add the green chillies and turmeric powder, and sauté for half a minute. Stir in the gram flour and sauté for one minute.
- Add the cooked colocasia leaves and half a cup of water if necessary and stir.
- Add the peanuts and more water if necessary. Cook for five minutes and add the jaggery. Bring to a boil again and stir in the remaining tamarind pulp.
- Add the coconut and some more water, if necessary. Cook on medium heat for half an hour, stirring occasionally. Serve hot.

Note: Alu is the Marathi word for colocasia.

SPINACH GNOCCHI

5 tablespoons spinach purée

6 medium potatoes

1 cup refined flour + for dusting

Salt to taste

8-10 black peppercorns, crushed

3 tablespoons olive oil

2 medium onions, chopped

5 garlic cloves, chopped

1 medium green capsicum, chopped

2 cups Tomato Concassé (page 95)

¼ cup cream

1 teaspoon dried oregano

2 tablespoons grated Parmesan cheese

5-6 fresh basil leaves, roughly torn

- Boil the potatoes, till just cooked. Drain, peel and mash while still hot. Cook the mashed potatoes in a pan so that all the excess moisture dries up.
- Add the refined flour, spinach purée, salt and one-fourth teaspoon crushed peppercorns and mix till smooth. Do not over-knead the dough. Divide the dough into four portions and shape each portion into a one-inch thick roll. Cut the roll into one-inch long pieces.

- Press each piece with the prongs of a fork to make a design and lightly roll in flour.
- Gently lower the gnocchi into a pan of boiling salted water and cook till they rise to the surface. Drain and refresh in chilled water. Drain again and stir in one tablespoon of olive oil and set aside.
- For the sauce, heat the remaining oil in a non-stick pan and sauté the onions, garlic and green capsicum.
- Add the tomato concassé and sauté for five minutes.
- Add three-fourth cup of water and bring the mixture to a boil. Stir in the cream, mix and bring to a boil again.
- Toss the gnocchi in the sauce, add salt, remaining crushed peppercorns and dried oregano.
- Sprinkle Parmesan cheese and the basil, and serve hot.

MOOLI KI SABZI

2 large white radishes with leaves
2 tablespoons mustard oil
2 pinches of asafoetida
1 teaspoon cumin seeds
Salt to taste
2 green chillies, chopped
½ teaspoon red chilli powder

- Scrape the radishes and chop finely. Chop the leaves finely as well.
- Heat the mustard oil in a non-stick *kadai* and add the asafoetida and cumin seeds.
- When the seeds begin to change colour, add the radishes with leaves, salt, green chillies and chilli powder.
- Stir-fry till the leaves soften slightly, but are still crunchy.
- Serve immediately.

PANEER KOFTE IN SPINACH CURRY

Kofte

200 grams cottage cheese, mashed

2 medium potatoes, boiled and mashed

3 tablespoons cornflour

½ teaspoon red chilli powder

½ inch ginger, finely chopped

Salt to taste

½ teaspoon white pepper powder

12-15 raisins, roughly chopped

12-15 cashew nuts, roughly chopped

Oil for deep-frying

Gravy

450 grams spinach, blanched

2 green chillies, roughly chopped

3 tablespoons oil

½ teaspoon caraway seeds

5-6 garlic cloves

½ cup tomato purée

½ teaspoon turmeric powder

1 teaspoon coriander powder

Salt to taste

1 teaspoon *garam masala* powder

¼ cup fresh cream

- In a bowl, mix together the mashed cottage cheese and potatoes, cornflour, chilli powder, ginger, salt to taste and white pepper powder. Divide the mixture into sixteen equal balls. Stuff each ball with chopped cashew nuts and raisins.
- Heat sufficient oil in a *kadai* and deep-fry the balls a few at a time until golden brown. Drain on absorbent paper and keep warm.
- In a blender, process the spinach and green chillies to a smooth purée.
- Heat three tablespoons of oil in a non-stick pan; add the caraway seeds and garlic, and stir-fry. Add the spinach purée and cook for about two to three minutes. Stir in the tomato purée and mix well. Add the turmeric powder, coriander powder and salt. Cook for four to five minutes.
- Add one cup of water and bring to a boil. Lower the heat and simmer for five to seven minutes. Stir in the *garam masala* powder and cook till the curry is reduced to half the original quantity.
- Stir in the cream and cook for half a minute. Remove from heat. Arrange the *kofte* in a serving dish. Pour the hot gravy on top and serve hot.

METHI ALOO

- 500 grams fresh fenugreek leaves, chopped
- 3 medium potatoes, halved and parboiled
- 2 tablespoons oil
- 1 teaspoon cumin seeds
- 1 teaspoon garlic, chopped
- 1 teaspoon ginger, chopped
- 2-3 dried red chillies, broken into pieces
- 2 large onions, sliced
- 1 teaspoon red chilli powder
- ½ teaspoon turmeric powder
- Salt to taste
- 1 teaspoon lemon juice

- Heat the oil in a pan; add the cumin seeds and when they begin to change colour, add the garlic and ginger, and sauté for half a minute. Add the red chillies and sauté for a minute. Add the onions and sauté till they turn translucent.
- Add the chilli powder and turmeric powder, and continue to sauté for half a minute. Add the parboiled potatoes and sauté for two to three minutes. Add the fenugreek leaves and stir to mix well.
- Cover and cook on medium heat till the potatoes are tender. Gently stir in the salt and lemon juice, and cook for one minute. Serve hot.

CHINESE GREENS WITH SOY SAUCE

- 10-12 spinach leaves, roughly torn
- 2 spring onions with greens, sliced
- 2-3 Chinese cabbage leaves, cut into 1-inch pieces
- ½ small broccoli, separated into small florets
- 4-6 French beans, cut diagonally into 1-inch pieces
- 1 medium green capsicum, cut into 1-inch diamonds
- 2 tablespoons oil
- 6-8 garlic cloves, crushed
- Salt to taste
- ½ teaspoon MSG (optional)
- 1 teaspoon sugar
- 1 teaspoon light soy sauce
- ¼ teaspoon white pepper powder
- 1 tablespoon cornflour
- 1 teaspoon toasted sesame seeds

- Blanch the broccoli and French beans in hot water for two to three minutes. Drain. Reserve some sliced spring onion greens for garnishing.
- Heat the oil in a non-stick wok; add the garlic and spring onions, and stir-fry for a few seconds.

- Add the broccoli, French beans and capsicum, and cook for two to three minutes.
- Stir in one and a half cups of water and simmer for a couple of minutes. Add the salt, MSG, sugar, soy sauce and white pepper powder, and stir.
- Add the spinach and Chinese cabbage. Stir in the cornflour mixed with one-fourth cup of water and cook, stirring, till the sauce thickens and coats the vegetables.
- Sprinkle toasted sesame seeds and serve hot, garnished with the reserved spring onion greens.

MOOLI SAAG

4 medium white radishes with leaves
Salt to taste
2 tablespoons oil
½ teaspoon mustard seeds
½ teaspoon cumin seeds

A pinch of asafoetida
½ teaspoon turmeric powder
1 teaspoon red chilli powder
1½ teaspoons sugar
1 teaspoon dried mango powder

- Chop the radishes into small pieces. Shred the leaves. Sprinkle a little salt on the radishes and set aside for twenty minutes. Drain the liquid.
- Heat the oil in a non-stick *kadai* and add the mustard seeds. When they begin to splutter add the cumin seeds and asafoetida, and sauté for half a minute.
- Add the turmeric powder and chilli powder, and sauté for ten seconds. Add the radishes with the leaves, and sauté for a minute.
- Sprinkle a little water to prevent scorching. Cover and cook on medium heat for ten minutes or till the radishes are soft and tender. Sprinkle the sugar and dried mango powder, and mix well. Adjust seasoning. Serve hot with *paranthe*.

SPINACH AND POTATO BHAJI

125 grams spinach, shredded

4 medium potatoes, cut into ½-inch cubes

2 tablespoons butter or oil

1 teaspoon red chilli powder

½ teaspoon cumin seeds

2 teaspoons coriander powder

¼ teaspoon turmeric powder

½ tablespoon lemon juice

Salt to taste

- Place the butter, chilli powder, cumin seeds, coriander powder and turmeric powder in a large microwave-safe bowl. Cook, uncovered, on HIGH (100%) for two minutes.
- Add the potatoes with half a cup of water and stir well. Cook, covered, on HIGH (100%) for ten to fifteen minutes.
- Add the spinach and cook on HIGH (100%) for two minutes.
- Stir in the lemon juice and salt, and serve hot.

METHI TAMATAR PANEER

250 grams fresh fenugreek leaves
4 medium tomatoes, finely chopped
200 grams cottage cheese, cut into ½-inch cubes
2-3 green chillies
1 inch ginger
6 garlic cloves

1 tablespoon oil
2 medium onions, finely chopped
1 tablespoon Kashmiri red chilli powder
1 tablespoon coriander powder
Salt to taste
1 teaspoon dried mango powder

- Grind together, the green chillies, ginger and garlic to a paste. Heat the oil in a non-stick pan; add the chopped onions and sauté for three to four minutes or till they just start turning brown. Add the ginger-garlic-green chilli paste, stir-fry for a few seconds and add the chilli powder, coriander powder and salt to taste. Mix well.

- Immediately, add the chopped fenugreek and cook on medium heat, stirring continuously for six to eight minutes, or until completely cooked and dry. Add the tomatoes, stir and cook over high heat for two to three minutes.

- Add half a cup of water, cover and simmer for three to four minutes. Add the cottage cheese; sprinkle dried mango powder and mix well. Cook till the cottage cheese is heated through, and serve immediately.

SOPPINA PALYA

700 grams amaranth leaves, chopped

2 tablespoons roasted peanuts, coarsely powdered

1 tablespoon oil

1 teaspoon mustard seeds

8-10 garlic cloves

4 dried red chillies, broken into bits

15-20 curry leaves

Salt to taste

- Heat the oil in a non-stick pan; add the mustard seeds, garlic, red chillies and curry leaves and sauté till fragrant. Add the amaranth leaves and stir.
- Cover and cook over medium heat till almost tender. Add the salt and cook till all the water evaporates. Set aside to cool slightly. Garnish with the powdered peanuts and serve.

Note: Soppu is the Kannada word for leafy vegetables.

MOOLYACHI BHAJI

- 4-5 medium white radish with leaves
- ¼ cup gram flour
- 2 tablespoons oil
- ½ teaspoon mustard seeds
- ¼ teaspoon asafoetida powder
- 1½ teaspoons split black gram
- 4 green chillies, finely chopped
- ¼ teaspoon turmeric powder
- Salt to taste
- ½ teaspoon sugar
- A few sprigs fresh coriander leaves, finely chopped

- Grate the white radish and finely chop the radish leaves. Dry-roast the gram flour in a non-stick pan on a low heat, stirring continuously, for three to four minutes.
- Heat the oil in a non-stick pan; add the mustard seeds and when they splutter, add the asafoetida powder and the split black gram. Stir-fry for a few seconds. Add the chopped green chillies, turmeric powder, radish, radish leaves, salt and the sugar.
- Mix well and cook, covered, for six to seven minutes on medium heat, stirring occasionally. When the radish is cooked and the mixture dries up, sprinkle the gram flour and continue to cook on medium heat for a couple of minutes, stirring occasionally. Serve hot, garnished with chopped coriander.

CHAKVATACHI BHAJI

- 1 bunch *chakvat*, finely shredded
- ¼ cup split Bengal gram
- ¼ cup peanuts
- 2 tablespoons oil
- 1 teaspoon cumin seeds
- ¼ teaspoon asafoetida
- 4 green chillies, finely chopped
- A pinch of sugar
- Salt to taste
- 3 tablespoons gram flour
- ½ cup buttermilk
- A few sprigs of fresh coriander, finely chopped

- Wash and soak the split Bengal gram in half a cup of water for an hour. Drain. Roast the peanuts and crush them roughly. Heat the oil in a non-stick pan; add the cumin seeds and sauté till they change colour. Add the asafoetida, green chillies and *chakvat* and stir-fry for a few minutes.
- Add the soaked gram, sugar and salt, mix well and cook till the gram is soft but firm. Mix together the gram flour and buttermilk till smooth and add to the pan. Cook for another five to six minutes stirring frequently. Serve hot, garnished with chopped coriander.

***Note:** Chakvat is the Marathi word for wild spinach.*

SARSON DA SAAG

4 cups fresh mustard leaves, chopped

2 cups spinach leaves (optional), chopped

1 cup *bathua* leaves (optional), chopped

4 tablespoons pure ghee

2 medium onions, chopped

2 inches ginger, chopped

6-8 garlic cloves, chopped

4-6 green chillies, chopped

1 teaspoon red chilli powder

Salt to taste

2 tablespoons cornflour

2 tablespoons butter

- Heat two tablespoons of ghee in a non-stick pan; add the onions and sauté till light brown. Add the ginger, garlic and green chillies, and sauté for a few minutes longer.
- Add the chilli powder, mustard leaves, spinach leaves and *bathua* leaves, and continue to sauté for a couple of minutes.
- Add the salt and cook on medium heat for ten minutes. Add the cornflour and a little water, and cook till the greens are soft.
- Cool slightly and transfer the mixture to a blender and process to a slightly coarse mixture.
- Heat the remaining ghee and butter in the same pan. Add the ground mixture and cook for five to ten minutes. Serve hot with *makki di roti*.

Chef's Tip
Traditionally *sarson da saag* is pounded to a paste with a wooden *mathni* or *ravai*, while it is being cooked. The process is quite cumbersome and time-consuming, but the result is delicious.

CABBAGE WITH CHANA DAL

1 medium cabbage, shredded

½ cup split Bengal gram

2 tablespoons oil

½ teaspoon mustard seeds

A pinch of asafoetida

1 teaspoon turmeric powder

4-6 curry leaves

2-3 green chillies, cut into two pieces

Salt to taste

1 teaspoon sugar

2 tablespoons grated coconut

A few sprigs of fresh coriander leaves, chopped

- Soak the split Bengal gram in one and a half cups of water for one hour.
- Heat the oil in a non-stick *kadai* and, add the mustard seeds. When they begin to splutter, add the asafoetida, turmeric powder, curry leaves and green chillies.
- Add the soaked gram and sauté for a few seconds. Sprinkle some water over the gram, cover and cook till half-done. Stir in the shredded cabbage, salt and sugar. Cover and cook till tender.
- Serve, garnished with the grated coconut and chopped coriander.

SAI BHAJI

- 400 grams spinach
- ½ medium bunch *khatta bhaji*
- 4 tablespoons oil
- ½ teaspoon cumin seeds
- 2 medium onions, finely chopped
- 1 inch ginger, finely chopped
- 3-4 green chillies, finely chopped
- 2 small long brinjals, cut into 1-inch cubes
- 2 medium potatoes, peeled and cut into 1-inch cubes
- 4 tablespoons split Bengal gram, soaked
- 2 large tomatoes, roughly chopped
- ¼ teaspoon turmeric powder
- 1 teaspoon red chilli powder
- Salt to taste

- Cut the spinach and half the *khatta* leaves into fine shreds.
- Heat the oil in a pressure cooker and add the cumin seeds. When they begin to change colour, add the onions and sauté till golden brown.
- Add the ginger and green chillies, and sauté for a few seconds. Add a little water, if required.
- Add the spinach, whole *khatta* leaves, shredded *khatta* leaves, brinjal and potato cubes, soaked Bengal gram, tomatoes, turmeric powder, chilli powder and salt. Stir in two cups of water.
- Seal the cooker with the lid and cook on high heat till the pressure is released once (one whistle). Lower the heat and cook for eight to ten minutes longer. Remove the lid when the pressure is released completely.
- Remove the potato cubes with a slotted spoon and blend the remaining mixture with a hand blender. Add the potato cubes, mix and serve hot.

Note: Khatta bhaji is the Hindi word for roselle leaves.

STEAMED LAUKI AND PALAK KOFTE

Kofte

250 grams bottle gourd, grated

450 grams spinach, blanched and chopped

Salt to taste

3 medium potatoes, boiled and mashed

2-3 green chillies, finely chopped

1 tablespoon raisins

3 tablespoons coarse rice powder

½ teaspoon *chaat masala*

½ teaspoon ginger paste

½ teaspoon garlic paste

1 large onion, finely chopped

2 tablespoons chopped fresh coriander

Gravy

½ teaspoon ginger paste

½ teaspoon garlic paste

1 large onion, finely chopped

1 teaspoon red chilli powder

¼ teaspoon turmeric powder

½ teaspoon *garam masala* powder

1 teaspoon dried fenugreek leaves, roasted and powdered

5-6 medium tomatoes, puréed

1½ tablespoons honey

Salt to taste

- Add the salt to the grated bottle gourd and set aside for five minutes. Squeeze the bottle gourd to remove the excess water. Squeeze out the excess water from the spinach.
- Mix the bottle gourd and spinach together with, the potatoes, green chillies, raisins, rice powder, *chaat masala*, ginger paste, garlic paste, chopped onion and salt in a large bowl.
- Divide into twenty equal portions and shape into oval *kofte*. Steam them in a steamer for fifteen to twenty minutes. Set aside.
- For the gravy, heat a non-stick pan. Roast the ginger paste, garlic paste and chopped onion on medium heat for five to six minutes. Add the chilli powder, turmeric powder, *garam masala* powder, dried fenugreek leaves and two tablespoons of water, and cook for a minute.
- Add the tomato purée, honey and salt. Add one cup of water and simmer for ten minutes. Arrange the steamed *kofte* on a serving plate, pour the gravy over and serve immediately, garnished with chopped coriander.

METHIWALI ARHAR DAL

125 grams fresh fenugreek leaves, chopped

1 cup split pigeon peas

½ teaspoon turmeric powder

Salt to taste

½ teaspoon red chilli powder

1 teaspoon grated jaggery

Seasoning

1 tablespoon pure ghee

¼ teaspoon asafoetida

6 garlic cloves

- Soak the split pigeon peas in two cups of water for one hour. Drain.
- Pressure-cook the split pigeon peas in three cups of water with the turmeric powder till the pressure is released four times (four whistles).
- Remove the lid when the pressure reduces completely and mash the *dal* well with the back of a ladle.
- Add half a cup of water, salt, chilli powder and jaggery, and bring to a boil.
- For the seasoning, heat the ghee in a small non-stick pan; add the asafoetida and garlic cloves. Sauté till the garlic turns light brown.
- Add the fenugreek leaves and sauté for one or two minutes. Pour the seasoning over the *dal* and stir well. Adjust the consistency by adding water if necessary.
- Serve hot.

PALAK KI KADHI

100 grams spinach, chopped
2 cups yogurt, whisked
4 tablespoons gram flour
2 tablespoons oil
1 teaspoon cumin seeds
½ teaspoon fenugreek seeds
A pinch of asafoetida

1 large onion, chopped
1 teaspoon ginger paste
3 green chillies, chopped
¼ teaspoon turmeric powder
½ teaspoon red chilli powder
Salt to taste
1 teaspoon sugar (optional)

- Whisk together the yogurt, gram flour and three cups of water till smooth. Heat the oil in a non-stick pan and add the cumin seeds and fenugreek seeds. When the seeds begin to change colour, add the asafoetida and onion, and sauté for two minutes.
- Add the ginger paste and green chillies, and sauté for half a minute. Add the turmeric powder, chilli powder and spinach, and sauté for two minutes. Add the yogurt mixture and bring to a boil. Add the salt and sugar, lower the heat and simmer for ten to fifteen minutes, or till the *kadhi* thickens. Serve hot.

KEERAI MILAKOOTAL

250 grams spinach, finely chopped
1½ cups split pigeon peas
½ medium coconut, grated
5 dried red chillies, broken into two
1 teaspoon cumin seeds
1 teaspoon skinless split black gram
Salt to taste
½ teaspoon turmeric powder
2 tablespoons oil
1 teaspoon mustard seeds
2 sprigs of curry leaves
¼ teaspoon asafoetida
10 shallots

- Wash the split pigeon peas, and soak in three cups of water for half an hour. Drain.
- Grind the coconut with the red chillies, cumin seeds and split black gram, to a fine paste.
- Pressure-cook the pigeon peas with three cups of water, salt and turmeric powder. Process in a blender when cool.
- Heat the oil in a non-stick pan. Add the mustard seeds, curry leaves and asafoetida.

- When the mustard seeds start to splutter, add the coconut paste and fry for three to four minutes.
- Add the shallots and the spinach, and stir-fry for two to three minutes.
- Add the *dal*, mix well and cook on low heat for ten minutes, stirring occasionally.
- Adjust the seasoning. Serve hot.

***Note:** Keerai is the Tamil word for spinach.*

PALAKWALI DAL

15-20 fresh spinach leaves, roughly shredded

¾ cup skinless split green gram

Salt to taste

1 teaspoon turmeric powder

2 tablespoons oil

A pinch of asafoetida

1 teaspoon cumin seeds

2 medium onions, chopped

2 green chillies, seeded and chopped

1 inch ginger, chopped

6-8 garlic cloves, chopped

1 teaspoon lemon juice

- Cook the split green gram with the salt, turmeric powder and five cups of water in a pressure cooker till the pressure is released twice (two whistles).
- Heat the oil in a non-stick *kadai*; add the asafoetida and cumin seeds. When the cumin seeds begin to change colour, add the onions and green chillies. Cook till the onions are soft and translucent. Add the ginger and garlic, and cook for half a minute.
- Add the *dal*, bring to a boil, and stir in the spinach and lemon juice. Simmer for two minutes and serve hot.

METHI CHAMAN BIRYANI

- 75 grams fresh fenugreek leaves
- 300 grams cottage cheese, cut into ½-inch cubes
- 1½ cups Basmati rice, soaked
- 1 cup sweetcorn kernels, blanched
- 1½ cups yogurt
- Salt to taste
- 1 teaspoon turmeric powder
- 2 tablespoons ginger paste
- 2 tablespoons garlic paste
- 2 green cardamoms
- 1 black cardamom
- 3-4 cloves
- 1 inch cinnamon
- 5-6 black peppercorns
- A generous pinch of saffron
- ½ cup warm milk
- 3 tablespoons ghee
- 2 large onions, sliced
- 2 green chillies, chopped
- 2 tablespoons coriander powder
- 1 tablespoon cumin powder
- 1 teaspoon red chilli powder
- 2 teaspoons *garam masala* powder
- 2 tablespoons chopped fresh coriander
- 2 inches ginger, cut into thin strips
- 10-12 fresh mint leaves
- ½ cup fried onion slices
- Wholewheat flour dough, to seal the pan

- Mix together the yogurt, salt, turmeric powder and one tablespoon each of ginger and garlic pastes in a bowl. Add the cottage cheese and corn, mix well and leave to marinate for about half an hour in a cool place.
- Cook the rice in four cups of boiling salted water, along with the green cardamoms, black cardamom, cloves, cinnamon and peppercorns till almost cooked. Drain and keep the rice warm.
- Soak the saffron in warm milk. Heat two tablespoons of ghee in a thick-bottomed non-stick pan. Add the onions and green chillies and sauté, stirring continuously, till the onions turn a light golden brown.
- Add the remaining ginger and garlic pastes, and mix well. Add the fenugreek leaves and cook over high heat for ten minutes, stirring continuously. Add the marinated cottage cheese and corn.
- Add the coriander powder, cumin powder and chilli powder, and mix thoroughly. Add the salt, half the *garam masala* powder and chopped coriander.
- Cook for five minutes over medium heat, stirring occasionally. Arrange half the cooked fenugreek leaves, corn and cottage cheese in a non-stick pan and spread

half the quantity of cooked rice on top. Sprinkle a little of the remaining *garam masala* powder, half the ginger strips, half the saffron-flavoured milk and mint leaves.

- Layer the remaining fenugreek leaves, cottage cheese and corn mixture on top of the rice, followed by the cooked rice.
- Sprinkle the remaining ginger strips, saffron-flavoured milk, *garam masala* powder and mint leaves on top.
- Melt the remaining ghee and drizzle it over the dish.
- Cover the pan with a lid and seal the edges with the wholewheat flour dough. Place the pan on a heated *tawa* and cook over low heat for fifteen minutes.
- Serve, garnished with fried onion slices and *raita*.

METHI MAKAI BIRYANI

½ cup fresh fenugreek leaves, chopped
½ cup sweetcorn kernels, boiled
1½ cups Basmati rice, soaked
1 tablespoon oil + for deep-frying
2 medium onions, sliced
1 bay leaf
4 cloves
7-8 black peppercorns
1 black cardamom
¾ cup sour yogurt
Salt to taste
1 teaspoon *garam masala* powder
1 inch ginger, cut into thin strips
2 tablespoons chopped fresh coriander

Masala Paste

2 medium onions, boiled
½ cup grated coconut
1½ inches ginger
4 garlic cloves
1 green chilli
1 teaspoon fennel seeds
1 teaspoon poppy seeds

- Drain and cook the rice in four cups of water with one teaspoon of oil till tender. Drain and set aside.
- Heat sufficient oil in a non-stick *kadai* and deep-fry the sliced onions till brown. Drain on absorbent paper. Grind all the ingredients for the *masala* paste.
- Heat one tablespoon of oil in a non-stick pan; add the bay leaf, cloves, peppercorns and black cardamom, and sauté till fragrant.
- Add the ground paste and sauté till golden brown. Add the yogurt, salt, fenugreek leaves and corn, and mix well. Add one cup of water if the mixture is too thick.
- Spread half the cooked rice in a layer in a separate thick-bottomed non-stick pan.
- Spread half the fenugreek-corn *masala* and sprinkle half the *garam masala* powder on top. Repeat the layers once more and top with the browned onions. Cover the pan with aluminium foil and place it on a hot *tawa*.
- Cook over low heat for about ten minutes. Uncover the pan just before serving and garnish with ginger strips and chopped coriander.
- Serve hot with *raita* and *papad*.

SPINACH AND MUSHROOM RISOTTO

125 grams spinach, roughly chopped
4-5 fresh button mushrooms, sliced
1½ cups arborio rice
5 tablespoons butter
1 medium onion, chopped
4-5 garlic cloves, chopped

1 cup white wine
3½ cups Vegetable Stock (page 95)
Salt to taste
¾ cup grated Parmesan cheese
½ teaspoon black pepper powder
½ cup cream

- Heat three tablespoons of butter in a pan. Add the onion, garlic and mushrooms, and sauté for two to three minutes. Add the rice, wine, half the vegetable stock and salt, and bring to a boil. Lower the heat and simmer for ten minutes.
- Stir in the remaining stock and cook for another ten minutes. Add the Parmesan cheese, pepper powder, spinach and cream, and mix well. Cook for two minutes and mix in the remaining two tablespoons of butter. Serve hot.

Chef's Tip
If arborio rice is not available use soaked parboiled rice.

TIRANGA KOFTA PULAO

1½ cups Basmati rice, soaked
3 tablespoons ghee
3 small onions, sliced
Salt to taste

Paneer Kofte
150 grams cottage cheese, grated
¼ teaspoon white pepper powder
½ teaspoon green cardamom powder
1½ tablespoons cornflour
Oil for deep-frying

Green Rice
200 grams spinach
1 green chilli
2 garlic cloves

White Rice
1 teaspoon cumin seeds

Yellow Rice
A few saffron threads

○ Mix the cottage cheese with the salt, white pepper powder and cardamom powder, and mash well. Divide into eighteen equal portions and shape into balls. Dust with cornflour. Heat sufficient oil in a *kadai* and deep-fry the cottage cheese balls till golden brown. Drain on absorbent paper. Boil the rice in four cups of

water till almost done; drain. Divide into three equal portions. For the green rice, blanch the spinach in plenty of water. Drain and purée in a blender along with the green chilli and garlic.

- Heat one tablespoon of ghee in a non-stick pan; add one-third of the onions and sauté till translucent. Add the spinach purée and sauté for one minute over high heat. Add one portion of the rice along with six cottage cheese balls and salt, and toss to mix. Transfer to a bowl and set aside.

- For the white rice, heat one tablespoon of ghee in a pan; add the cumin seeds and when they begin to change colour, add half the remaining onions and sauté till translucent. Add another portion of the rice, six cottage cheese balls and salt, and toss well. Transfer to a separate bowl and set aside.

- For the yellow rice, soak the saffron in two tablespoons of water. Heat one tablespoon of ghee in a non-stick pan, add the remaining onions and sauté till translucent. Add the remaining rice with the saffron-flavoured water. Add the remaining cottage cheese balls and salt, and toss to mix. Transfer to a bowl and set aside.

- To serve, in a transparent square glass dish, spread a layer of green rice and level the surface. Spread a layer of white rice over the green rice and level the surface. Top with a layer of yellow rice. Alternatively, arrange the rice in a pattern on a flat dish.

PALAK AUR PANEER PARANTHA

8-10 large fresh spinach leaves

1½ cups wholewheat flour

½ cup refined flour

Salt to taste

1 teaspoon sesame seeds

Ghee for shallow-frying

Stuffing

300 grams cottage cheese, grated

3 green chillies, chopped

1 tablespoon chopped fresh coriander

1 small onion, chopped

1½ teaspoons *chaat masala*

Salt to taste

- Sift the wholewheat flour and refined flour with salt into a bowl and set aside.
- Blanch the spinach leaves in boiling water for one minute. Drain, squeeze out the excess water and blend to a thick purée in a blender.
- Add the spinach purée and sesame seeds to the flour and knead with enough water into a soft dough. Cover the dough with a damp cloth and rest the dough for half an hour.
- For the stuffing, mix together the cottage cheese, green chillies, chopped coriander, onion, *chaat masala* and salt in a large bowl. Divide into eight equal portions.

- Knead the dough again and divide into eight equal portions. Shape into balls and press between your palms.
- Roll out each ball into a four-inch round and thin down the edges.
- Place one portion of the stuffing in the centre and gather the edges together and shape into a ball again. Roll out into a seven-inch round *parantha*.
- Heat a non-stick *tawa*. Place each *parantha* on it, turn over once and drizzle a little melted ghee around it.
- Turn it over again and spread a little more ghee on the other side. Cook till both sides are cooked.

METHI MAKAI PARANTHA

½ cup fresh fenugreek leaves, chopped

½ cup sweetcorn kernels, boiled and crushed

2 cups wholewheat flour

Salt to taste

4 tablespoons ghee

1 small onion, chopped

1 medium potato, boiled and mashed

2 tablespoons fresh coriander, chopped

2 green chillies, chopped

½ teaspoon carom seeds

1 tablespoon lemon juice

- Mix together the wholewheat flour and salt, and knead with enough water into a soft dough. Divide into eight equal portions and cover with a damp cloth for about fifteen minutes.
- Heat one tablespoon of ghee in a non-stick *kadai*; add the onion, corn and fenugreek leaves and sauté for a few minutes. Spread out on a plate to cool.
- Mix the sautéed mixture with the mashed potato. Add the chopped coriander, green chillies, carom seeds, lemon juice and salt, and mix well. Divide into eight equal portions.

- Roll out each portion of dough into a small *puri*, place a portion of stuffing in the centre, gather the edges together and roll into a ball. Roll out the ball into a five-inch round *parantha*.
- Heat a non-stick *tawa*, place the *parantha* on it and cook till light golden specks appear. Brush the top with a little ghee and turn it over. Cook the other side and brush with ghee.
- Serve hot.

ANNEXURE

Date And Tamarind Chutney

Wash, stone and chop 15-20 dates. Dry-roast 2 teaspoons cumin seeds and ¼ teaspoon fennel seeds. Cool and grind to a powder. Cook the dates, 1 cup tamarind pulp, cumin and fennel powder, ½ cup jaggery, 2 teaspoons red chilli powder, 1 teaspoon dried ginger powder, black salt, salt and four cups of water till thick.

French Dressing

Combine one tablespoon of olive oil, ¼ teaspoon each of paprika, salt, mustard powder, 1 teaspoon sugar and one tablespoon of vinegar or lemon juice in a bowl. Beat well with a wire whisk until smooth. Add two more tablespoons of olive oil and beat well again. Add one more tablespoon of vinegar or lemon juice, three more tablespoons of olive oil and one garlic clove. Mix well.

Place the dressing in a jar and store in a cool place. You may remove the garlic after six or seven days. Shake the dressing well before using.

Green Chutney

Grind together 1 cup fresh coriander, ½ cup fresh mint, 2-3 green chillies, black salt to taste, ¼ teaspoon sugar and 1 tablespoon lemon juice to a smooth paste using a little water if required.

- **Mayonnaise**
  Place 1 egg yolk, salt to taste, ¼ teaspoon each white pepper powder, French mustard and sugar and 1 teaspoon vinegar in a clean bowl and mix thoroughly with a whisk. Alternatively, process the mixture in a blender. Add 1 cup of oil, a little at a time, whisking or blending continuously, until all the oil is incorporated. Add 1 teaspoon lemon juice and adjust seasoning. Store in an airtight jar in a refrigerator.

- **Tomato Concassé**
  To make 1 cup of tomato concassé, blanch 5 medium tomatoes in plenty of boiling water for two minutes. Drain and refresh in cold water; peel, cut in half, remove seeds and chop roughly.

- **Tamarind Pulp**
  Soak 75 grams tamarind in 100 ml warm water for 10-15 minutes. Grind to a smooth paste and strain to remove any fibres. Store in an airtight container in the refrigerator.

- **Vegetable Stock**
  Peel, wash and chop 1 onion, ½ medium carrot, 2-3 inch celery stalk and 2-3 garlic cloves. Place in a pan with 1 bay leaf, 5-6 peppercorns, 2-3 cloves and 5 cups of water and bring to a boil. Lower heat and simmer for 15 minutes and strain. Cool and store in a refrigerator till further use.

GLOSSARY

English	Hindi	English	Hindi
Amaranth	Chouli	Gram, Bengal split	Chana dal
Asafoetida	Hing	Gram, black skinless split	Dhuli urad dal
Black peppercorns	Kali mirch	Gram, black split	Chilkewali urad dal
Button mushrooms	Khumb	Gram, green skinless split	Dhuli moong dal
Capsicum	Shimla mirch	Lettuce	Salad ke patte
Caraway seeds	Shahi jeera	Mustard	Rai
Cardamoms, green	Chhoti elaichi	Nutmeg	Jaiphal
Celery	Ajmud	Olives	Jaitun
Colocasia	Arbi	Poppy seeds	Khuskhus
Coriander powder	Dhania powder	Radish	Mooli
Cottage cheese	Paneer	Raisins	Kishmish
Dill	Suva	Refined flour	Maida
Drained (hung) yogurt	Chakka	Sesame seeds	Til
Dried fenugreek leaves	Kasoori methi	Spinach	Palak
Fennel seeds	Saunf	Split pigeon peas	Toovar dal/arhar dal
Fenugreek leaves	Methi	Vinegar	Sirka
Fresh parsley	Ajmoda	Walnuts	Akhrot
Gram flour	Besan	Wild spinach	Bathua